The Bible and Life

God's Message for Today

Joy P. Clarke

Augsburg Fortress, Minneapolis

Contents

INTERSECTIONS
Small Group Series

The Bible and Life
God's Message for Today

Developed in cooperation with the Division for Congregational Ministries

George S. Johnson, series introduction
David W. Anderson and Rich Gordon, editors
The Wells Group, series design
Skjold Photographs, cover photo

Scripture quotations are from New Revised Standard Version Bible, copyright 1989 Division of Christian Education of the National Council of the Churches of Christ in the United States of America. Used by permission.

ISBN 0-8066-0127-2
Printed on 50% recycled paper (10% postconsumer fibers)
Manufactured in U.S.A.

  3 4 5 6 7 8 9 0 1 2 3 4 5 6 7 8 9

Introduction

The Bible as a source of life

Years ago, when our daughter Akilah was about six years old, my husband and I sat down to play a card game with her. We played carelessly, assuming that parents would easily win against a six-year-old. Instead, our daughter beat us terribly, so we asked, "How in the world did you do that, dear?" Akilah smiled and said, "I read the instructions!"

The Bible is not simply a book of instructions, nor is it a manual that can tell us how to approach every life situation. Still, it is God's Word, which means that it is a source of life. It has the power to affect our lives. It has the power to create faith. Those who read the Bible and listen to or study its words will find direction for living, and they will find much more — hope, peace, forgiveness, grace, courage, and a sense of being connected to the people of God in every generation.

Akilah knew how to win her card game: Read the instructions! Her discovery is a good lesson for those who want to have a more vibrant and informed faith. God's Word in Scripture is available today in a huge array of versions and formats. It is the world's best-selling book of all time, but too often it gathers dust on our bookshelves. According to Genesis 3, we human beings have always been trying to take control of our own destiny, trying to make sense of life on our own. But hard as we try, we cannot master life. We wonder why we so often feel desperate, unhappy, unfulfilled, or anxious.

This is exactly why God's Word exists. It reminds us of our limitations (we are not God!) and shows us how we get off track. This is God's Law at work. But thanks be to God, it also shows us why we have reason to hope. God sent Jesus to forgive those who were thought to be unforgivable, to love those who were thought to be unlovable. One of the most familiar verses of the Bible puts it so clearly: "God so loved the world that he gave his only Son, so that everyone who believes in him may not perish but may have eternal life" (John 3:16). This is the Gospel, the good news of Jesus Christ.

The purpose of this study

The aim of this study is to explore how God's Word in Scripture (the Bible) can make a difference in our lives and in our faith. But it can only make a difference if we read it and study it, and open ourselves to all its potential gifts.

You can get a Bible and start reading it on your own. Unfortunately, we often begin our personal study with good intentions but then stop after a few days. An even better way for you to study the Bible is to do it with a small group of people. From the start, the Bible has existed in order to tell the story of God's people. Stories can only "work" when they are shared. The same is true of the Bible. When we share its stories, it "works" on us. It helps us make sense of our own personal stories and gives us the power and courage to reshape our lives. And it reminds us that this power of new life is not something we create, but rather it comes to us through the Holy Spirit. The Bible, which contains the Gospel, is one of the gifts that God's Spirit uses to teach us.

Another great gift that God's Spirit uses to enlighten us is the community of faith — other people who are struggling with the same issues you face but always in the context of what it means to be faithful. God's Word can also come to us through the words and the stories shared by others. That's a primary reason this small group ministry study is made available to you.

When you bring together a study of God's Word in Scripture with the supportive "witness" of other people of faith, you have a powerful combination.

Maybe a few people at your workplace would be interested in meeting once a week. Maybe some of your neighbors would like to form a group and meet in someone's home. Your local church is a good place to find interested people. When we study the Bible with a small group, we're more likely to keep going in our Christian reflection. Attending weekly meetings will help us to become more disciplined in our study, and sharing ideas and stories with the group members will make studying the Bible more lively and enjoyable. We may even start a new or deeper friendship along the way.

The chapter themes in this study

1. The Bible: Its Principle Purpose
The Bible is God's Word, a means by which Jesus comes to us.

2. The Bible: Its Inspiration and Interpretation
Jesus Christ, the Word made flesh, was both human and divine. The Bible also has this dual nature. It is inspired by God but created by human beings who were moved by the Spirit to provide a message within a given historical and cultural context.

3. The Bible: God's Gift for Guidance
The Bible challenges us to look at who we are and to seek God's guidance for our daily lives.

4. The Bible: Promise and Fulfillment
The Bible records the promises and the undeserved kindness of God at work in both the Old Testament and the New Testament, especially through Jesus Christ.

5. The Bible: Source of Life
The Bible provides resources for study, meditation, and prayer, which God uses to strengthen our faith and empower us for daily living.

6. The Bible: A Tool for Witness
The Bible provides a story that we are called to share with others.

A few things to consider

You may find it helpful to spend more than one session working with a particular chapter. If your time together is relatively short (an hour or less), you are not likely to get through every section and certainly not through every question. The point of a small group is not to rush through content. Take time to let the Word and your own sharing "work on" you.

During each session, remember my grandmother's advice: Don't be afraid to ask questions that you think make you look stupid. Usually, if you don't understand something, somebody else doesn't understand it either. Also, remember this saying from the Ewe tribe in Africa about the good sense of people studying together in small groups: "Two foolish heads are better than one."

SMALL GROUP SERIES

Welcome into the family of those who are part of small groups! Intersections Small Group Series will help you and other members of your group build relationships and discover ways to connect the Christian faith with your everyday life.

This book is prepared for those who want to make a difference in this world, who want to grow in their Christian faith, as well as for those who are beginning to explore the Christian faith. The information in this introduction to the Intersections small group experience can help your group make the most out of your time together.

Biblical encouragement

"Do not be conformed to this world, but be transformed by the renewing of your minds, so that you may discern what is the will of God—what is good and acceptable and perfect" (Romans 12:2).

Small groups provide an atmosphere where the Holy Spirit can transform lives. As you share your life stories and learn together, God's Spirit can work to enlighten and direct you.

Strength is provided to face the pressures to conform to forces and influences that are opposed to what is "good and acceptable and perfect." To "be transformed" is an ongoing experience of God's grace as we take up the cross and follow Jesus. Changed lives happen as we live in community with one another. Small groups encourage such change and growth.

What is a small group?

A number of definitions and descriptions of the small group ministry experience exist throughout the church. Roberta Hestenes, a Presbyterian pastor and author, defines a small group as an intentional face-to-face gathering of three to twelve people who meet regularly with the common purpose of discovering and growing in the possibilities of the abundant life.

Whatever definition you use, the following characteristics are important.

Small—Seven to ten people is ideal so that everyone can be heard and no one's voice is lost. More than 12 members makes genuine caring difficult.

Intentional—Commitment to the group is a high priority.

Personal—Sharing experiences and insights is more important than mastering content.

Conversational—Leaders that facilitate conversation, rather than teach, are the key to encouraging participation.

Friendly—Having a warm, accepting, non-judgmental atmosphere is essential.

Christ-centered—The small group experience is biblically based, related to the real world, and founded on Christ.

Features of Intersections Small Group Series

A small group model

A number of small group ministry models exist. Most models include three types of small groups:

- *Discipleship groups*—where people gather to grow in Christian faith and life;

- *Support and recovery groups*—which focus on special interests, concerns, or needs; and

- *Ministry groups*—which have a task-oriented focus.

Intersections Small Group Series presently offers material for discipleship groups and support and recovery groups.

For discipleship groups, this series offers a variety of courses with Bible study at the center. What makes a discipleship group different from traditional group Bible studies? In discipleship groups, members bring their life experience to the exploration of the biblical material.

For support and recovery groups, Intersections Small Group Series offers topical material to assist group members in dealing with issues related to their common experience, hurt, or interest. An extra section of facilitator helps in the back of the book will assist leaders of support and recovery groups to anticipate and prepare for special circumstances and needs that may arise as group members explore a topic.

Ministry groups can benefit from an environment that includes prayer, biblical reflection, and relationship building, in addition to their task focus.

Four essentials

Prayer, personal sharing, biblical reflection, and a group ministry task are part of each time you gather. These are all important for Christian community to be experienced. Each of the six chapter themes in each book includes:

- Short prayers to open and close your time together.

- Carefully worded questions to make personal sharing safe, non-threatening, and voluntary.

- A biblical base from which to understand and discover the power and grace of God. God's Word is the compass that keeps the group on course.

- A group ministry task to encourage both individuals and the group as a whole to find ways to put faith into action.

Flexibility

Each book contains six chapter themes that may be covered in six sessions or easily extended for groups that meet for a longer period of time. Each chapter theme is organized around two to three main topics with supplemental material to make it easily adaptable to your small group's needs. You need not use all the material. Most themes will work well for 1½- to 2-hour sessions, but a variety of scheduling options is possible.

Bible based

Each of the six chapter themes in the book includes one or more Bible texts printed in its entirety from the New Revised Standard Version of the Bible. This makes it easy for all group members to read and learn from the same text. Participants will be encouraged through questions, with exercises, and by other group members to address biblical texts in the context of their own lives.

User friendly

The material is prepared in such a way that it is easy to follow, practical, and does not require a professional to lead it. Designating one to be the facilitator to guide the group is important, but there is no requirement for this person to be theologically trained or an expert in the course topic. Many times options are given so that no one will feel forced into any set way of responding.

Group goals and process

1. Creating a group covenant or contract for your time together will be important. During your first meeting, discuss these important characteristics of all small groups and decide how your group will handle them.

Confidentiality—Agreeing that sensitive issues that are shared remain in the group.

Regular attendance—Agreeing to make meetings a top priority.

Non-judgmental behavior—Agreeing to confess one's own shortcomings, if appropriate, not those of others, and not giving advice unless asked for it.

Prayer and support—Being sensitive to one another, listening, becoming a caring community.

Accountability—Being responsible to each other and open to change.

Items in your covenant should be agreed upon by all members. Add to the group covenant as you go along. Space to record key aspects is included in the back of this book. See page 60.

2. Everyone is responsible for the success of the group, but do arrange to have one facilitator who can guide the group process each time you meet.

The facilitator is not a teacher or healer. Teaching, learning, and healing happen from the group experience. The facilitator is more of a shepherd who leads the flock to where they can feed and drink and feel safe.

Remember, an important goal is to experience genuine love and community in a Christ-centered atmosphere. To help make this happen, the facilitator encourages active listening and honest sharing. This person allows the material to facilitate opportunities for self-awareness and interaction with others.

Leadership is shared in a healthy group, but the facilitator is the one designated to set the pace, keep the group focused, and enable the members to support and care for each other.

People need to sense trust and freedom as the group develops; therefore, avoid "shoulds" or "musts" in your group.

3. Taking on a group ministry task can help members of your group balance personal growth with service to others.

In your first session, identify ways your group can offer help to others within the congregation or in your surrounding community. Take time at each meeting to do or arrange for that ministry task. Many times it is in the doing that we discover what we believe or how God is working in our lives.

4. Starting or continuing a personal action plan offers a way to address personal needs that you become aware of in your small group experience.

For example, you might want to spend more time in conversation with a friend or spouse. Your action plan might state, "I plan to visit with Terry two times before our next small group meeting."

If you decide to pursue a personal action plan, consider sharing it with your small group. Your group can be helpful in at least three ways: by giving support; helping to define the plan in realistic, measurable ways; and offering a source to whom you can be accountable.

5. Prayer is part of small group fellowship. There is great power in group prayer, but not everyone feels free to offer spontaneous prayer. That's okay.

Learning to pray aloud takes time and practice. If you feel uncomfortable, start with simple and short prayers. And remember to pray for other members between sessions.

Use page 61 in the back of this book to note prayer requests made by group members.

6. Consider using a journal to help reflect on your experiences and insights between meeting times.

Writing about feelings, ideas, and questions can be one way to express yourself; plus it helps you remember what so often gets lost with time.

The "Daily Walk" component includes material that can get your journaling started. This, of course, is up to you and need not be done on any regular schedule. Even doing it once a week can be time well spent.

How to use this book

The material provided for each session is organized around some key components. If you are the facilitator for your small group, be sure to read this section carefully.

The facilitator's role is to establish a hospitable atmosphere and set a tone that encourages participants to share, reflect, and listen to each other. Some important practical things can help make this happen.

- Whenever possible meet in homes. Be sure to provide clear directions about how to get there.

- Use name tags for several sessions.

- Place the chairs in a circle and close enough for everyone to hear and feel connected.

- Be sure everyone has access to a book; preparation will pay off.

Welcoming

Small groups can successfully meet in many different locations, such as a home, church, park, or restaurant. They can even meet in a different location for each session and still reach the course goals. However, any space selected should:
- be a quiet area free from noise and interferences;
- be adequately warm and dry;
- include comfortable seating;
- include a table large enough for materials and refreshments.

In addition to the New Revised Standard Version (NRSV) Bible, it may be helpful to have other versions of the Bible on hand for the sake of comparison.

Above all, seek to make all who enter your group feel valued and welcome. Extend the hand of friendship and study and discuss together in an atmosphere of acceptance and respect. Remember, no question is a silly question. Since small groups can be a place for sharing some private thoughts, make sure that you agree together that this is a place where thoughts can be shared without fear that they will be quickly broadcast outside the group.

Focus

Each of the six chapter themes in this book has a brief focus statement. Read it aloud. It will give everyone a sense of the direction for each session and provide some boundaries so that people will not feel lost or frustrated trying to cover everything. The focus also connects the theme to the course topic.

Community building

This opening activity is crucial to a relaxed, friendly atmosphere. It will prepare the ground for gradual group development. Two "Community Building" options are provided under each theme. With the facilitator giving his or her response to the questions first, others are free to follow.

One purpose for this section is to allow everyone to participate as he or she responds to non-threatening questions. The activity serves as a check-in time when participants are invited to share how things are going or what is new.

Make this time light and fun; remember, humor is a welcome gift. Use 15 to 20 minutes for this activity in your first few sessions and keep the entire group together.

During your first meeting, encourage group members to write down names and phone numbers (when appropriate) of the other members, so people can keep in touch. Use page 59 for this purpose.

Discovery

This component focuses on exploring the theme for your time together, using material that is read, and questions and exercises that encourage sharing of personal insights and experiences.

Reading material includes a Bible text with supplemental passages and commentary written by the topic writer. Have volunteers read the Bible texts aloud. Read the commentary aloud only when it seems helpful. The main passage to be used is printed so that everyone operates from a common translation and sees the text.

"A Further Look" is included in some places to give you additional study material if time permits. Use it to explore related passages and questions. Be sure to have your own Bible handy.

Questions and exercises related to the theme will invite personal sharing and storytelling. Keep in mind that as you listen to each other's stories, you are inspired to live more fully in the grace and will of God. Such exchanges make Christianity relevant and transformation more likely to happen. Caring relationships are key to clarifying one's beliefs. Sharing personal experiences and insights is what makes the small group spiritually satisfying.

Most people are open to sharing their life stories, especially if they're given permission to do so and they know someone will actively listen. Starting with the facilitator's response usually works best. On some occasions you may want to break the group into units of three or four persons to explore certain questions. When you reconvene, relate your experience to the whole group. The phrase "Explore and Relate," which appears occasionally in the margin, refers to this recommendation. Encourage couples to separate for this smaller group activity. Appoint someone to start the discussion.

Wrap-up

Plan your schedule so that there will be enough time for wrapping up. This time can include work on your group ministry task, review of key discoveries during your time together, identifying personal and prayer concerns, closing prayers, and the Lord's Prayer.

The facilitator can help the group identify and plan its ministry task. Introduce the idea and decide on your group ministry task during "Wrap-up" time in the first session. Tasks need not be grandiose. Activities might include:

- Ministry in your community, such as "adopting" a food shelf, clothes closet, or homeless shelter; sponsoring equipment, food, or clothing drives; or sending members to staff the shelter.

- Ministry to members of the congregation, such as writing notes to those who are ill or bereaved.

- Congregational tasks where volunteers are always needed, such as serving refreshments during the fellowship time after worship, stuffing envelopes for a church mailing, or taking responsibility for altar preparations for one month.

Depending upon the task, you can use part of each meeting time to carry out or plan the task.

In the "Wrap-up," allow time for people to share insights and encouragements and to voice special prayer requests. Just to mention someone who needs prayer is a form of prayer. The "Wrap-up" time may include a brief worship experience with candles, prayers, and singing. You might form a circle and hold hands. Silence can be effective. If you use the Lord's Prayer in your group, select the version that is known in your setting. There is space on page 62 to record the version your group uses. Another closing prayer is also printed on page 62. Before you go, ask members to pray for one another during the week. Remember also any special concerns or prayer requests.

Daily walk

Seven Bible readings and a thought, prayer, and verse for the journey related to the material just discussed are provided for those who want to keep the theme before them between sessions. These brief readings may be used for devotional time. Some group members may want to memorize selected passages. The Bible readings can also be used for supplemental study by the group if needed. Prayer for other group members can also be part of this time of personal reflection.

A word of encouragement

No material is ever complete or perfect for every situation or group. Creativity and imagination will be important gifts for the facilitator to bring to each theme. Keep in mind that it is in community that we are challenged to grow in Jesus Christ. Together we become what we could not become alone. It is God's plan that it be so.

For additional resources and ideas see *Starting Small Groups—and Keeping Them Going* (Minneapolis: Augsburg Fortress, 1995).

1 The Bible: Its Principal Purpose

Focus

The Bible is God's Word, a means by which Jesus comes to us to offer new life.

Community building

Arrange your seating in a circle for introductions in the whole group.

- Begin by dividing your group into pairs. Spend about three minutes telling each other your names, your expectations for this study on the Bible, and one thing people wouldn't know about you if you didn't tell them. Then spend about 10 minutes introducing each other to the whole group. Close your introduction of your partner by completing this thought: "My wish for you is . . . "

For setting small group goals, see page 7.

List your goals and commitments in the appendix on page 60 for future reference.

- Good small groups don't just happen. They will flourish if group members focus on respect, honesty, openness, concern, and commitment. It is important to set some goals for your group before you begin. You will all feel more comfortable together if you know and agree to live by expectations that are shared by all.

Option

Share one of your earliest memories of reading the Bible or seeing it being read. What thoughts and feelings are associated with that memory? Are they similar to your thoughts and feelings regarding the Bible today? Explain.

- Spend a few minutes sharing your expectations for this small group. Consider things such as shared leadership, confidentiality, meeting length and space, refreshments, and additional things that will affect your time together. List your goals and expectations on page 60.

Opening prayer

Gracious God, we thank you for the gift of Scripture and for the opportunity to study your Word. Guide us as we meet together and open our minds and hearts to receive the promise of new life that Jesus brings. Amen.

A Living Word

Consider these questions before looking at the biblical text. Discuss in pairs or groups of three.

- What does it mean to say that "words can give life or snatch it away"?

- How has this been true in your life?

- What is the most important "word" in your life at this moment?

John 1:1-5,14-17

1 In the beginning was the Word, and the Word was with God, and the Word was God. 2 He was in the beginning with God. 3 All things came into being through him, and without him not one thing came into being. What has come into being 4 in him was life, and the life was the light of all people. 5 The light shines in the darkness, and the darkness did not overcome it.

14 And the Word became flesh and lived among us, and we have seen his glory, the glory as of a father's only son, full of grace and truth. 15 (John testified to him and cried out, "This was he of whom I said, 'He who comes after me ranks ahead of me because he was before me.'") 16 From his fullness we have all received, grace upon grace. 17 The law indeed was given through Moses; grace and truth came through Jesus Christ.

Discuss as a group.

This text reminds us that God's Word can be defined in more than one way. The Word is Scripture (the Bible), but it is also Jesus Christ, God's Son, the Word made flesh. The Word lives as Christ and comes alive through the Holy Spirit. Without Jesus, the words printed in your Bible are mere words. Without the Spirit, they lie dormant and lifeless.

God's Word, then, is both Jesus himself and the means by which we come to know him and his promises. Martin Luther descibed Scripture as the manger that cradles Christ. Just as the shepherds and wise men came to the stable to see the baby Jesus, we come to Scripture to see Jesus, but we see more than an infant king. We see his whole life and we see his promises in relation to the whole history of God and God's people.

- If you were to try and explain John 1:1-5 to someone who had never read the Bible or who had heard little about Jesus, what would you say?

- Using the language of John the Baptist in 1:15, how do you think Scripture "testifies" to Jesus Christ?

■ What does it mean that we receive "grace upon grace" from the fullness of Christ?

Explore and relate.
Explore in groups of three or four; then *relate* a brief summary to the entire group.

Consider this

The hymn "Your Word, O Lord, Is Gentle Dew," has three stanzas. Each stanza begins by giving a different image of God's Word. Choose one of these images and relate your thoughts about what the statement means to you.

"Your Word, O Lord, is gentle dew . . ."
"Your Word is like a flaming sword . . ."
"Your Word [is] a wondrous star . . ."

■ What other images might you add to this list?

A further look

Read and discuss.

Look again at John 1:17. This verse provides a kind of summary of the purposes for the Old and the New Testaments. The Old Testament tells the story of God's people, the Israelites (Jews), and much of it is devoted to discussing the Law of Moses and the people's efforts to live up to it. The New Testament focuses on the person and work of Jesus.

Unfortunately, the testaments sometimes get defined as all Law (Old) and all Gospel (New). This is simply not true. The Old Testament reveals God as One who both judges and forgives, punishes and loves. In fact, the promises that find fulfillment in Jesus Christ are born in God's covenants with Israel and preached by the Old Testament prophets. What's more, the New Testament contains its share of Law, which forces us to look carefully at who we really are and challenges us to live faithfully.

■ When you were a child or youth, what was your primary image of God?

Choose one and explain.

a. Angry judge	d. Mysterious force
b. Loving savior	e. Parent
c. Teacher	f. Other

■ What was your primary image of the Bible?
   a. A big dusty book that was hard to understand.
   b. Something that people read in church.
   c. A book of rules telling you how to live.
   d. A story book filled with interesting characters.
   e. Other.

John 5:39-40

³⁹ [Jesus said] "You search the scriptures because you think that in them you have eternal life; and it is they that testify on my behalf. ⁴⁰ Yet you refuse to come to me to have life."

These two verses are from a long speech Jesus made in John 5 after he healed a man on the Sabbath. According to the Law of Moses, healing on the Sabbath broke the laws regarding "no work" on this Jewish holy day. So some in the crowd got angry at Jesus for breaking this commandment. But when he referred to God as his Father, some began to make plans to kill him (5:16-18). Sensing their anger and resentment, Jesus defended himself and his actions (5:19-47).

Discuss as a group.

■ The two verses printed above focus on the purpose of the scriptures. According to Jesus, for what reason did the people search the scriptures (5:39)? What could be wrong with that?

■ Teachers in Israel, like the Pharisees, argued that the way to eternal life was through obeying the Law of Moses. How does this fact shed light on Jesus' comment in 5:39?

■ Jesus implies in 5:40 that eternal life could be found in him, not simply in the scriptures (what we call the Old Testament). What would have been threatening about such a statement to those who were in the crowd? Who might have heard Jesus' words as a "freeing" thing, a message of hope?

If this first study is used for more than one small group session, introduce subsequent sessions with a "Community Builder" and "Prayer" and end with "Wrap-up."

■ We have the privilege of living after the resurrection. We have the full witness of both the Old and New Testaments. With this in mind, read 5:39-40 again. Now what do you think of Jesus' statements? Do they still ring true, or do you want to modify his words? Why or why not?

Consider this

So far we have said that Jesus is the "Word of God." That's important because so many people tend to think of the Bible alone as God's Word.

Choose one and explain.

■ How do you think of Jesus?
   a. Friend   c. Savior   e. King
   b. Teacher   d. Healer   f. Other

Discuss as a group.

Discovery

The Vine and its branches

The Bible is a means by which God's love reaches out to us. In it we discover Christ, the living Word. At the same time, Christ comes to us through the Bible in order to bring new life. This is the Bible's key purpose.

Think of a tomato seed or small tomato plant. What is its purpose? Why does it exist?

Jesus has a purpose for those who call themselves his followers. He talks about the purpose in the following verses.

John 15:4-5,16-17

4 **Abide in me as I abide in you. Just as the branch cannot bear fruit by itself unless it abides in the vine, neither can you unless you abide in me.** 5**I am the vine, you are the branches. Those who abide in me and I in them bear much fruit, because apart from me you can do nothing.**

16**You did not choose me but I chose you. And I appointed you to go and bear fruit, fruit that will last, so that the Father will give you whatever you ask him in my name.** 17**I am giving you these commands so that you may love one another.**

Discuss as a group.

- In this passage, who is the vine and who are the branches?

- What does Jesus mean when he says, "You did not choose me but I chose you"? Why is this distinction so important?

- Think about how fruit grows. From where does it get its nutrients, its ability to grow and produce? How is this like the relationship Jesus describes here in John 15?

- What is Jesus' purpose for us (John 15:16-17)? Can this happen apart from the presence of Scripture in your life? Why or why not?

Respond to these quotes as a group.

Consider this

"Our task is not to search for God, but rather to open ourselves to the reality of God's search for us."

From *Gospel-Centered Spirituality*, copyright © 1990 Augsburg Fortress.

"The Bible is not only for information but for transformation."

The power to love

When Jesus commands us to love others (John 15:17), he is not asking us to do this on our own. We can love because he abides in us.

- What things get in the way of showing the kind of love Jesus describes?

- I have trouble showing love toward . . .

- If I could make better use of my time, I could use that time to show God's love to others by . . .

Discuss as a group.

Consider this

In the book *High Speed Healing*, one doctor writes, "If I told patients to raise their blood levels of immune globulins or killer T-cells, no one would know how. But if I can teach them to love themselves and others fully, the same changes happen automatically."

From *High-Speed Healing*, ed. William LeGro (Emmaus, PA: Rodale Press, Inc., 1991), 334.

A further look

In Luke 15:11-32, Jesus tells the story of a family—a father and two sons. The younger son asks for his share of his father's wealth, then quickly leaves home. After a time of foolish living, he is hungry, broke, and miserable.

Finally, he decides to go home and face his father and beg for mercy. To his surprise, the father welcomes him back to the family with open arms and no questions asked.

It is Jesus whom we meet through the Bible and who calls us to see ourselves for who we are. It is Jesus who reveals that God is our loving Father, always ready to receive us when we turn to God for forgiveness and help. It is Jesus who gives us the power to turn back to God, to give our life meaning and purpose.

Often Jesus comes to us through God's Word in Scripture. That makes the Bible a treasure that finds us and brings us new life.

Explore and relate.

- If I could start my life over again tomorrow, I would . . .
- Two things I learned in this session are . . .
- Share a time when you have been embraced by God's love.

Wrap-up

See page 10 in the introduction for a description of "Wrap-up."

Before you go, take time for the following:

- **Group ministry task**

- **Review**

- **Personal concerns and prayer concerns**

Ongoing prayer requests can be listed on page 61. See page 62 for suggested closing prayers.

- **Closing prayers**

Daily walk

Bible readings

Day 1
John 15:4-5

Day 2
John 15:6-7

Day 3
John 15:10

Day 4
Matthew 28:19-20

Day 5
Exodus 33:14

Day 6
Isaiah 43:2

Day 7
Matthew 18:20

Thought for the journey

We are connected to God through Jesus and through God's Word in Scripture. We are also connected to all God's people in every generation, including those who wrote Scripture and those who seek to interpret it anew in this day.

Prayer for the journey

Almighty God, we thank you for sending your son, Jesus, to us. Please let him abide in us each day. May your Spirit help us to see Jesus in Scripture just as he has seen us and called us his own.

Verse for the journey

"Where two or three are gathered in my name, I am there among them" (Matthew 18:20).

2 The Bible: Inspiration and Interpretation

Focus

Jesus Christ, the Word made flesh, is both human and divine. The Bible also has this dual nature. It is inspired by God and written by human beings who were moved by the Spirit to provide God's message within a given historical and cultural context.

Community building

Many people are happy in the work they do, but once in a while it is fun to dream about other options.

Work in pairs for 5 minutes.

- Each person writes down on a piece of paper an occupation they might like to have (other than one they have had or are in). Retired people can write down a job they wished they could have had. Fold these papers so they cannot be read.

- Choose a partner. Each person tries to guess the partner's occupation by asking a maximum of 10 questions that can only be answered with "Yes" or "No." After both have taken turns questioning, write down your guess.

- Gather together as a group in a circle. One pair at a time, compare guesses with the actual occupation. How many different occupations are represented in the group?

Option
Try playing the Telephone Game for a few minutes. One person should write a sentence or two on a piece of paper. That person whispers a sentence to the next person, who in turn whispers it to the next person, and so on. The last person repeats the sentence aloud, so the group can compare it with the original.

- **Did the message change? If so, why?**

- **What does this activity say about how we communicate?**

Opening prayer
Dear Lord, thank you for preserving your written word through past centuries so that we may study it in our time. Please guide our understanding of Scripture today. Amen.

The inspired Word of God

What does it mean to say that the "Bible is inspired by God"? It's not an easy question. It has caused major debates in the history of the church. Volumes have been written on the subject. We don't have the room to discuss all the issues here, but we can make a start.

Choose any or all that you think apply. Discuss your responses together.

■ I think the statement, "The Bible is the inspired Word of God," means:
   a. The Bible is completely true.
   b. The people who wrote the Bible wrote down God's words just like a secretary takes dictation from a tape recording.
   c. The Bible is the story of God's involvement with the world, especially humankind.
   d. The Bible's message has the power to give new life.
   e. God's Holy Spirit wrote the words of the Bible on the minds of the human writers.
   f. Human writers saw the presence of God at work in the events of human history and wrote it down as a witness to later generations.

Few subscribe to the idea that the writers of the Bible were merely recording God's words like a secretary transcribes dictation from a tape recorder. Even so, some would like to believe this is true in order to remove the "human element" from the writing of Scripture. But that would make the Bible completely divine. That would go against the nature of God, who came to us in human form to both tell and be the good news, the gospel.

The Bible is certainly true, but when we try to equate truth and inspiration, sometimes the focus shifts from the overall truth and power of the message to arguing about whether each specific test is literally true in every situation or trying to prove where and how an event actually occurred. But these are concerns for interpretation, which we will explore later.

The Bible is both divine and human. God's Spirit inspired the biblical writers just as the Spirit continues to inspire preachers and teachers, prophets and poets today. But the writers lived in a particular time. They read the signs around them and recognized how God was at work in their lives and in historic events. The truth of their observations has been proven through history and confirmed by the tradition, that is, by faithful followers in each generation.

1 Corinthians 13:12

Read aloud.

12 For now we see in a mirror, dimly, but then we will see face to face. Now I know only in part; then I will know fully, even as I have been fully known."

2 Timothy 3:14-16

14 But as for you [Timothy], continue in what you have learned and firmly believed, knowing from whom you learned it, 15 and how from childhood you have known the sacred writings that are able to instruct you for salvation through faith in Christ Jesus. 16 All scripture is inspired by God and is useful for teaching, for reproof, for correction, and for training in righteousness.

Paul's words in 1 Corinthians 13:12 were written in the context of talking about spiritual gifts. Even after talking about how God's Holy Spirit inspires people to preach and teach and prophesy and speak in tongues (1 Corinthians 12), he focused on love as the greatest gift of all (1 Corinthians 13). In the midst of this discussion, he reminded his readers that God and God's message are still cloaked in mystery. Things that seem important to us in life may not really be important at all. Things that seem to be one way may really be much different. It's as if we're looking at life into a cloudy mirror. We're not seeing clearly. Our sight, our understanding, is limited by our sin and by just being human. We can't see as God sees.

Discuss as a group.

- What do Paul's words suggest to you about the inspiration of Scripture?

- What danger did Paul seem to be guarding against in 13:12?

- How can we abuse the power of God's Spirit? Have you ever seen this happen? Can you think of examples?

While we want to acknowledge our human inadequacies and even failures when it comes to knowing and carrying out God's purposes, 2 Timothy reminds us to have confidence that the Scriptures are inspired by God.

- According to 2 Timothy 3:15, what is the purpose of the sacred writings?

- In addition, what is Scripture useful for (13:16)?

- What is the most inspiring thing about Scripture for you?

Consider this

Some people turn to the Bible because they have faith. Others begin to read it because they are looking for faith. Both read the Bible for good reasons. The books of the Bible were written and preserved by communities of believers to nurture people in the faith.

From *A Beginner's Guide to Reading the Bible*, copyright © 1991 Augsburg Fortress.

■ What does it mean to say that the Bible is a book of faith?

A further look

We can agree that God has inspired the words in the Bible and we also acknowledge that human beings wrote the original words, and dedicated translators and copyists labored long and hard to produce Bible manuscripts in many different languages. Their work, too, was inspired, but it was and still is filtered through human writers and translated from one language to another. The process of translating and recopying texts had to be influenced by differences in human experience and perception, to say nothing of working by candlelight in cold rooms for hours at a time. Still, we have to marvel at the way God's Word in Scripture has survived to the present.

■ Why do you think there are so many different Bible translations today? In your opinion, is it good to have so many translations? Why or why not?

The "Verse for the journey" (page 18) for the last chapter theme was Matthew 18:20. Take a moment to read it.

■ What important role can a group play in studying the Bible? Why might group study be better than individual study?

■ Why is prayer important when reading and studying Scripture?

■ When I read the Bible I usually:
    a. Feel confident I know what it means.
    b. Am confused and don't see how it fits together.
    c. Get answers to my questions.
    d. Am seeking God's will in my life.
    e. Other.

The powers of observation

Provide paper and pencils or pens.

Try this experiment. Ask one person in the group to volunteer to be the "actor." The actor needs to perform a task of his or her own choosing. The task should take about 30 seconds. The actor may say something while doing the task, but does not have to speak. The rest of the group will observe what the actor is doing and saying.

Spend 5 minutes creating a summary.

After the task is completed, the group members will each write a summary of what the actor did. These summaries can be simple or detailed. The more detail you add, the more unique the various "interpretations" of the action will be. Then read the summaries aloud.

- How and why did the summaries vary?

- What does this say to you about human observation?

Interpreting God's Word

Remember, if this study is used for more than one small group session, introduce subsequent sessions with a "Community Builder" and "Prayer" and end with "Wrap-up."

The interpretation of God's Word began with the biblical writers themselves. Before manuscripts were ever written down, much of the basic information found in the Bible began as oral information—stories, sayings, wisdom. These were passed on for generations. The biblical writers took this information and put it into a form that made sense. Remember, their intention was not to write detailed historic accounts but to provide key information that would create faith in the reader or support a particular view of God's action in history.

For example, many scholars say that the Bible contains two accounts of creation (Genesis 1:1—2:4a and Genesis 2:4b—25) that were written by two different writers at two different times in history. Now, the key content is the same in each— God is creator and we are God's creatures, but many of the details vary in each version. What accounts for this difference? Interpretation. Each writer knew the basic story, but the details are the writer's own. He or she did not try to put his or her particular situation, life experience, and context on the shelf. It influenced the written "telling" of a story that had existed in oral form for a long time.

- How does it strike you that even the biblical writers may have been interpreting God's Word even as they wrote it down?

The gospels also are a good place to look for how the different writers reported similar events. For example, look at these passages that describe the death of Jesus:

Matthew 27:46,50

46 And about three o'clock Jesus cried with a loud voice, "Eli, Eli, lema sabachthani?" that is, "My God my God, why have you forsaken me?" . . . 50 Then Jesus cried again with a loud voice and breathed his last.

Luke 23:46

46 Then Jesus, crying with a loud voice, said, "Father, into your hands I commend my spirit." Having said this, he breathed his last.

John 19:30

30 When Jesus had received the wine, he said, "It is finished." Then he bowed his head and gave up his spirit.

Discuss as a group.

- What differences do you see in these accounts of Jesus' death?

- What might account for these differences?

These differences don't make one author right and another one wrong. It does show that the Bible was created by different individuals with varying perspectives. We can't know all the influences that shaped each of the biblical writers. We can only observe the differences in their written record and speculate about why they exist. This kind of observation helps us to think about what the text may have meant to the original readers or listeners. But what does the text mean to us (to me)? That's the next task of interpretation.

In Context

To find out what the Bible says, we have to read it. But finding out what the Bible means is a different task. Interpretation is affected by a number of things that fall under the wide heading of "context." Our context takes into account things like our culture and ethnic backgrounds, our personal "histories" and our present life situations—things like work, family, and crises. That means that interpreting the Bible is never done in a vacuum or void.

Here's an example. Our Bible class was discussing Exodus 23:19: "The choicest of the first fruits of your ground you shall bring into the house of the LORD your God." Most class members were raised in an urban area and interpreted the passage as a command from God to wear our best clothes to church, and to buy the best altar linens, candle holders, and robes that money could buy.

Eddie Cohen, however, was raised on a farm, and he said, "But on our farm, even the choicest of the first fruits were not necessarily the best of the season's crop. Many times, the second and third harvests had better quality fruits or vegetables. Maybe the passage is emphasizing the idea that we should think of God first in doing our budget rather than emphasizing the quality of our clothes or our candle holders."

Explore and relate.

■ Where and how were you raised? How do you think your background affects how you interpret the Bible?

■ What are some of the most important influences in your life—past and present?

■ How do you interpret Exodus 23:19?

Discuss as a group.

■ Which of the following statements are helpful reminders regarding the interpretation of Scripture?

Choose any that apply and add your own.

    a. Be careful not to read individual verses out of context.
    b. What it meant to the original readers has nothing to do with what a passage means to me (us).
    c. The Bible was inspired by God but written by people.
    d. Be careful not to interpret Bible passages just to suit your own needs.
    e. Seek the guidance of the Holy Spirit through prayer.
    f. Friends, pastors, and resources like books can help us interpret the meaning of Scripture.
    g. The Bible is always in the process of being reinterpreted.
    h. Add your own reminders here.

A further look

Read Ephesians 5:22.

■ Taken literally, without looking at the rest of this passage from Ephesians or at any cultural differences between first-century Palestine and late twentieth-century North America, how would you interpret this passage?

■ Now read Ephesians 5:21-28. How do these verses help you put 5:22 in context? Does it make a difference in how you interpret Ephesians 5:22? If so, how?

■ How might someone's life situation affect how he or she interprets this passage? List some possibilities.

Wrap-up

See page 10 in the introduction for a description of "Wrap-up."

Before you go, take time for the following:

- ■ **Group ministry task**

- ■ **Review**

Ongoing prayer requests can be listed on page 61. See page 62 for suggested closing prayers.

- ■ **Personal concerns and prayer concerns**

- ■ **Closing prayers**

Daily walk

Bible readings

Day 1
2 Peter 1:20-21

Day 2
2 Timothy 3:1-16

Day 3
Matthew 25:37-40

Day 4
Isaiah 40:8

Day 5
Jeremiah 36:2

Day 6
Job 32:8

Day 7
Matthew 12:50

Thought for the journey

The Bible is a gift of life given to us by God's own Spirit and through the toil of numerous writers and translators. Interpreting the Bible is an exciting and fulfilling task that helps us to seek meaning for our lives.

Prayer for the journey

Lord, our Creator, we thank you for speaking to us through the Bible. Please help us to hear you more clearly. In Jesus' name we pray. Amen.

Verse for the journey

"Your words were found, and I ate them, and your words became to me a joy and the delight of my heart; for I am called by your name, 0 LORD, God of hosts" (Jeremiah 15:16).

3 The Bible: Its Gift for Guidance

The Bible challenges us to look at who we are and to seek God's guidance.

Community building

Provide several pairs of scissors and a variety of written materials such as a comic book, newspaper, an outrageous tabloid ("Space Aliens Take Over City Hall!"), magazines, an old children's book, a medical journal, or a tax form.

- Ask each group member to cut a section of a page from any of the publications provided. These sections should be equal in size, about 6" x 6".

- Then put all the sections in a bag. Let each person pull one item from the bag, and see if the group can identify which publication each section came from.

- The Bible is something like this "grab-bag" of different kinds of literature. Just like each type of material was created to provide information and to teach or shed light on something, the Bible also is a teaching tool. One common thread that runs through the various of types of literature is the thread of wisdom and guidance.

- How do you know what kind of material you are reading?

- How many different types of literature might be found in the Bible? Give it a try. Don't worry if you are not totaly accurate. The point is to start thinking about the variety that exists.

Option

Spend about 10 minutes discussing the following as a group.

Name your favorite kind of written material and tell why it is your favorite. Then name one type of written material you don't like to read, and why.

Opening prayer

Almighty God, We thank you for your Word. May it draw us ever closer to you, and may it be a light for our paths. Grant us insight as we study. In Jesus' name we pray. Amen.

Psalm 1:1-2

Read and discuss as a group.

1 Happy are those who do not follow the advice of the wicked, or take the path that sinners tread, or sit in the seat of scoffers; 2but their delight is in the law of the LORD, and on his law they meditate day and night.

Psalm 119:105

105 Your word is a lamp to my feet and a light to my path.

The first two verses of Psalm 1 provide a kind of summary of a key theme in the Bible and in the Jewish faith. Those who follow the law of the Lord will prosper; those who don't will perish (Psalm 1:6). It seems so simple. Follow the rules and God will reward you. Don't follow them and you will be punished, or excluded from being part of God's people.

This was a theme that dominated the Jewish religion at the time of Jesus. The Jewish leaders and teachers had established a rather complicated set of laws for the religious and social life of the Jewish people. These laws were based on the Law of Moses, which is what the first five books of Jewish Scripture—Genesis, Exodus, Leviticus, Numbers, and Deuteronomy—are called. They said that following the Law of Moses was the way of salvation for the Jewish people. The problem is, the Law was being used not only in a positive way to give the people a clear identity and encourage them to live in harmony, it was also excluding certain people from being included in God's people. It was used to identify good people and bad people, righteous and sinners, and keep the two apart.

- Have you ever seen God's Law or the Bible used primarily as a way to identify sins and sinners? Explain.

- In the church, do you think God's law is emphasized (too much/not enough/about right)? Explain.

- All 176 verses of Psalm 119 focus on the same theme as Psalm 1—the goodness of God's law and the joy that comes from following it. In 119:105, God's Word is basically synonymous with the Law. What images are used to describe the Law (Word)? What does this verse mean to you?

- What other images can you think of to describe how God's law functions?

A further look

Read and discuss.

The most familiar of the Old Testament's laws is probably the Ten Commandments. They contain laws that define the people's relationship with God and their relationship with one another.

■ How many could you name without looking at the list? Check out how you did by looking at Exodus 20:1-17 or Deuteronomy 5:6-21.

■ When you think of the Ten Commandments, do you think of them as:

Choose one and explain.

    a. a gift from God.
    b. a burden that causes guilt.
    c. unrealistic expectations.
    d. something that would change the world if everyone followed them.
    e. rules to follow in order to gain God's approval and blessing.
    f. Other.

■ What difference does it make how you view the laws that God gave to the people of the Old Testament?

Discovery

Matthew 5:17

17 [Jesus said] "Do not think that I have come to abolish the law or the prophets; I have come not to abolish but to fulfill."

Romans 3:21-24,28,31

21 But now, apart from law, the righteousness of God has been disclosed, and is attested by the law and the prophets, 22the righteousness of God through faith in Jesus Christ for all who believe. For there is no distinc-

tion, 23since all have sinned and fall short of the glory of God; 24they are now justified by his grace as a gift, through the redemption that is in Christ Jesus. . . . 28For we hold that a person is justified by faith apart from works prescribed by the law. . . . 31Do we then overthrow the law by this faith? By no means! On the contrary, we uphold the law.

The New Testament has been described by some as telling the story of a family argument. The family is the Jewish people, and one of the major arguments was over whether or not following the Law of Moses could make a person righteous, or right with God. Jesus was a Jew, and so was Paul, the apostle who wrote Romans. You can see by these passages that both saw the law as a useful thing, not something to be thrown out or treated lightly.

Discuss as a group.

■ What did Jesus say about the law?

■ What did he mean when he said he came to "fulfill the law"?

Choose one and explain.

    a. He followed the law perfectly, so we would have a standard to live up to.
    b. He satisfied the demands of the law so that we might be free from having to follow it in order to gain God's favor.
    c. Now, laws are no longer necessary.
    d. The law can't save anyone, only Jesus can.
    e. Other.

■ According to Paul (Romans 3), how are we "justified" or made righteous (right with God)?

■ Many Jewish teachers taught that a person could be saved, made righteous in God's eyes, by following the Law of Moses. Paul himself had been a Pharisee, an expert in the Law of Moses. But an encounter with Jesus (Acts 9) changed his thinking. According to Romans 3:23, why couldn't the Law justify?

■ How does it make you feel to know that following God's law is not how you become acceptable to God or gain salvation?

    a. Disappointed   d. Relieved
    b. Confused   e. Thankful
    c. Free   f. Other

Consider this

"I discovered that it is not on our forgiveness any more than on our goodness that the world's healing hinges, but on [God's]. When [God] tells us to love our enemies, [God] gives, along with the command, the love itself."

Corrie ten Boom in *The Hiding Place* (Chosen Books, Inc. 1971, p. 238).

■ What do you make of Corrie ten Boom's comment?

■ Can you relate it to the discussion of the biblical texts on the previous page? If so, how?

A further look

The Bible does indeed offer guidance for living, but that statement can so easily be turned in the wrong direction. People can use it to emphasize that God gave the law in order to show us how we can make ourselves righteous. But Paul said that the law could never be a means of justification. He argued from the beginning that God justifies people by faith (Romans 4). And this faith that justifies is not our work but God's work in us, given in the Word (Romans 10:5-13).

So what is the law good for? First, it establishes an order to life so that we are able to receive the promises and blessings of God. The laws of God are given in order to protect us from one another and establish an environment where justice and concern prevail.

Second, the law found in God's Word is like a mirror. When we look into it we see who we really are, which means we realize we can't rely on ourselves or our ability to obey the law for salvation.

■ Given what you have read and discussed so far, how would you complete this sentence: "The Bible is a gift of guidance because . . .

Discovery

In a variety of forms

■ If you were trying to convince someone that your love for them is beginning to overwhelm you, which of the following forms of literature would you use:

    a. a biological description of heart tissue.

    b. a love poem.

    c. a business letter.

The biblical writers realized that certain forms of writing were suited to different messages. *Psalms*—poems that were sometimes put to music—were used in worship. *Stories* like Ruth usually were told to provide information, but also to make a particular point or advance a position. Jesus used a particular form of story, the *parable*, to teach about the kingdom of God. *Wisdom sayings* like the *proverbs* were intended to teach about practical matters or give advice. *Prophetic speeches* brought God's Word as in the form of judgment or promise. *Laws or commands* laid out how the people were to live together in the presence of God. *History writings* recalled the important facts of Israel's history, the life of Jesus (gospels), or the early church (Acts). A number of books in the New Testament are *epistles*, letters written to churches or individuals stating the good news of Jesus Christ and addressing a way of life consistent with the gospel.

All these forms, in their own way, were written to illumine and to guide readers to a deeper understanding of God and God's interaction with humankind. What's more, they move beyond the transmission of knowledge to create faith.

Listed below are examples of different forms of biblical literature. Read them and determine the following for each example:

    a. What kind of literature is it? (Refer to the italicized words identified above.)
    b. Why do you think it was written? OR What was the author's purpose? You may look at the other verses that are near it to get a better idea of its context.
    c. What does it say to me?

Read the biblical texts. Discuss as a group.

Deuteronomy 6:4-7

4 Hear, O Israel: The LORD is our God, the LORD alone. 5 You shall love the LORD your God with all your heart, and with all your soul, and with all your might. 6 Keep these words that I am commanding you today in your heart. 7 Recite them to your children and talk about them when you are at home and when you are away, when you lie down and when you rise.

Psalm 27:1

1 The LORD is my light and my salvation; whom shall I fear? The LORD is the stronghold of my life; of whom shall I be afraid?

Proverbs 12:25

25 Anxiety weighs down the human heart, but a good word cheers it up.

Isaiah 11:1-2

[1] A shoot shall come out from the stump of Jesse, and a branch shall grow out of his roots. [2] The Spirit of the LORD shall rest on him, the spirit of wisdom and understanding, the spirit of counsel and might, the spirit of knowledge and the fear of the LORD.

Matthew 13:44

[44] "The kingdom of heaven is like treasure hidden in a field, which someone found and hid; then in his joy he goes and sells all that he has and buys the field."

Acts 6:7

[7] The word of God continued to spread; the number of the disciples increased greatly in Jerusalem, and a great many of the priests became obedient to the faith.

Philippians 1:1-2

[1] Paul and Timothy, servants of Christ Jesus, To all the saints in Christ Jesus who are in Philippi, with the bishops and deacons: [2] Grace to you and peace from God our Father and the Lord Jesus Christ.

Mark 2:1-2

[1] When he returned to Capernaum after some days, it was reported that he was at home. [2] So many gathered around that there was no longer room for them, not even in front of the door; and he was speaking the word to them.

Explore and relate.

- As a result of this experience, one new thing I learned or was emphasized for me is . . .

- This insight can help my appreciation and study of the Bible by . . .

Wrap-up

Before you go, take time for the following:

- Group ministry task

- Review

- Personal concerns and prayer concerns

- Closing prayers

Daily walk

Bible readings

Day 1
Ecclesiastes 3:1-22

Day 2
Micah 6:6-8

Day 3
Ecclesiastes 5:10-17

Day 4
Mark 12:28-34

Day 5
1 John 4:7-21

Day 6
Ephesians 2:8-10

Day 7
Romans 12:2

Thought for the journey

As we study God's word, God can change hopelessness to hope.

Prayer for the journey

Lord, thank you for the members of this group. Please help us to learn to love your Word in all its richness and variety. In Jesus' name. Amen.

Verse for the journey

"For whatever was written in former days was written for our instruction, so that . . . we might have hope" (Romans 15:4).

4 The Bible: Promise and Fulfillment

Focus

The Bible reveals God's promises to humanity in both the Old and New Testaments. The life, death, and resurrection of Jesus fulfills God's promises and is the foundation of our faith and hope.

Community building

- Sit in a circle with the rest of the group. A volunteer will describe a second group member in one sentence without mentioning the second member's name. Let one person guess who is being described (one guess). If the guess is incorrect, the volunteer gives one more sentence. One more group member makes a guess. If necessary, the volunteer gives a third and final clue. If the group still can't guess correctly, the volunteer is the winner and tells the group who was being described. The winner also chooses the next person to be "It."

- What kinds of qualities can we use to describe people without mentioning their names?

Option

Each person writes his or her name on a slip of paper, folds it several times and places it in a bowl or paper bag. Divide the group into two teams. Each team takes a turn. One team member selects a folded paper, reads the name silently, and then tries to give one-word clues to her or his teammates to help them guess the name on the paper. The team that takes the least amount of time to guess correctly wins.

- What describes us best—our past, our present circumstances, or our expectations and hopes for the future?

Opening prayer

Almighty God, we thank you for your grace and blessing throughout the ages. Please help us to trust your promises. In Jesus' name. Amen.

Promises, promises

Think about it—much of life is built around promises. In our work and in our families, in our church and in other social relationships, much of what we say and do revolves around making and keeping promises.

- In your life, name some ways that promises come into play.

- What are the three most important promises you have ever made?

- When someone makes a promise to me, I . . .

- When someone breaks a promise to me, I . . .

- What is the most important promise anyone ever made to you?

Genesis 12:1-3

1 Now the LORD said to Abram, "Go from your country and your kindred and your father's house to the land that I will show you. 2 I will make of you a great nation, and I will bless you, and make your name great, so that you will be a blessing. 3 I will bless those who bless you, and the one who curses you I will curse; and in you all the families of the earth shall be blessed."

Genesis 17:1,5-8,15-16

1 When Abram was ninety-nine years old, the LORD appeared to Abram, and said to him, . . . 5 No longer shall your name be Abram, but your name shall be Abraham; for I have made you the ancestor of a multitude of nations. 6 I will make you exceedingly fruitful; and I will make nations of you, and kings shall come from you. 7 I will establish my covenant between me and you, and your offspring after you. . . . 8 And I will give to you, and to your offspring after you, the land where you are now an alien, all the land of Canaan, for a perpetual holding; and I will be their God. . . . 15 As for Sarah your wife, you shall not call her Sarai, but Sarah shall be her name. 16 I will bless her, and moreover I will give you a son by her. I will bless her, and she shall give rise to nations; kings of peoples shall come from her."

God made numerous promises in the Old Testament. One of the key promises was the agreement (covenant) that God made with Abraham and Sarah. Much of the rest of the Old Testament tells the story of how God worked to fulfill these promises to the chosen people, Israel, in spite of their frequent attempts to turn their backs on God and their failure to hold up their end of the agreement—to remain faithful to God alone.

■ What exactly did God promise to Abraham and Sarah?

Both Abraham and Sarah laughed at the promise (see 17:17-18; 18:12-15), a laugh that did not go unnoticed by God. God told Abraham to name the child Isaac, which means, "he laughs."

■ What does this story, filled with promises and laughter, suggest about the promise?

■ What does it say about God's relationship with us?

Explore and discuss in pairs.

Share promise proverbs with the whole group.

Consider this

"A life without promise is a life without hope."

■ What is your reaction to this quote?

■ Try creating your own "promise proverb," a one-sentence truism about promises.

A further look

Read and discuss.

Another key set of promises involved the future of King David's descendants. David was regarded as Israel's greatest king. Many would argue that the promises God made to Abraham and Sarah came to fullest bloom during David's reign. After David's death, his son Solomon became king. Though he was wise and wealthy and built the first temple, his decision to allow the building of idols to foreign gods began a series of events that eventually spelled defeat and exile for the people of Israel. Though some of the people eventually returned to rebuild Jerusalem and the temple, they only controlled their own land and destiny for brief periods in the 500 years before Jesus was born.

Read the promise God made to David through the prophet Nathan in 2 Samuel 7:4-17.

■ What promises did God make to David in this text?

■ In Luke 1:26-33, the promise is fulfilled in Jesus. What does this promise and fulfillment say to you about God? About us?

David was certainly not a perfect human being. 2 Samuel 11 tells the story of how David ordered a soldier named Uriah to fight in the front lines of a battle, virtually ensuring that he would be killed. David wanted to get rid of Uriah so he could have Bathsheba, Uriah's wife. In spite of this sin, God still chose to fulfill the promises made to David.

- What does this say to you about God?

- What does this mean for you?

Discovery

Luke 24:27

27 Then beginning with Moses and all the prophets, he interpreted to them the things about himself in all the scriptures.

In the last chapter we looked at Matthew 5:17, where Jesus said he had come to fulfill the law and the prophets, that is, the Jewish Scriptures, which Christians call the Old Testament.

Discuss as a group.

- Jesus is never mentioned by name in the Old Testament. What point, then, does he make in Luke 24:27?

Luke 4:16-21

16 When [Jesus] came to Nazareth, where he had been brought up, he went to the synagogue on the sabbath day, as was his custom. He stood up to read, 17 and the scroll of the prophet Isaiah was given to him. He unrolled the scroll and found the place where it was written: 18 "The Spirit of the Lord is upon me, because he has anointed me to bring good news to the poor. He has sent me to proclaim release to the captives and recovery of sight to the blind, to let the oppressed go free, 19 to proclaim the year of the Lord's favor." 20 And he rolled up the scroll, gave it back to the attendant, and sat down. The eyes of all in the synagogue were fixed on him. 21 Then he began to say to them, "Today this scripture has been fulfilled in your hearing."

- What did Jesus identify as his mission?

■ What does this mean for you?
   a. Jesus sets us free through forgiveness.
   b. Jesus heals those who are hurting and disabled.
   c. Jesus loves the poor but hates the rich.
   d. Jesus cares about outcasts or the powerless.
   e. Jesus calls us to reach out to those who are less fortunate than ourselves.
   f. Other.

Consider this

**He did not wait till the world was ready,
till men and nations were at peace.
He came when the Heavens were unsteady,
and prisoners cried out for release.**

**. . . He came to a world which did not mesh,
to heal its tangles, shield its scorn.
In the mystery of the Word made Flesh
the Maker of the stars was born.**

**We cannot wait till the world is sane
to raise our shouts with joyful voice,
for to share our grief, to touch our pain,
He came with Love: Rejoice! Rejoice!**

From "First Coming" in *A Cry Like a Bell* by Madeleine L'Engle (Wheaton, IL: Harold Shaw Publishers, © 1987 by Crosswicks)

■ How does this poem strike you?

■ How does it relate to the themes of promise and fulfillment?

A further look

There is no question that the writers of the New Testament saw Jesus as the fulfillment of promises made especially by the Old Testament prophets, but also revealed in other Old Testament Scriptures as well. The Gospel of Matthew uses this formula or some version of it many times: "All this took place to fulfill what had been spoken by the Lord through the prophets." This formula is then followed by a passage from the Old Testament as they relate to the promised Messiah, which these writers believed was Jesus.

■ Match the following New Testament passages with the Old Testament passage that it is interpreted as fulfilling.

Old Testament	New Testament
___ Micah 5:2	a. Hebrews 8:6-12
___ Isaiah 53:3	b. Matthew 13:34-35
___ Genesis 3	c. Matthew 2:14
___ Hosea 11:1	d. John 1:11
___ Psalm 78:2	e. Matthew 1:20-23
___ Isaiah 7:13-14	f. Romans 5:12-19
___ Jeremiah 31:31-34	g. Matthew 2:1

These are only a handful of examples. As you read more of the New Testament, look for how the writers use the Old Testament to point out that Jesus is the fulfillment of God's promises.

■ How does Jesus fulfill God's promises in your life?

Discovery

Yesterday, today, tomorrow

Promise and fulfillment are linked to time. Human life itself is marked by significant events that are related to time—birth, growth, marriage, retirement, and death.

Consider and discuss.

■ Here are some examples of important biblical themes. When you think of these, do you think of them in terms of being related to PAST, PRESENT, or FUTURE? Be careful, as some may need more than one answer.

Label each term as PAST, PRESENT, and/or FUTURE.

_____ Creation
_____ Fall (sin)
_____ Forgiveness
_____ Promise and fulfillment
_____ New life
_____ Judgment
_____ Redemption (salvation)

■ When you look at your own past, present, and future, what do you see? What would you change, if anything?

Discovery

Revelation 21:1,3-4

¹ Then I saw a new heaven and a new earth; for the first heaven and the first earth had passed away, and the sea was no more.

³ And I heard a loud voice from the throne saying, "See, the home of God is among mortals. He will dwell with them as their God; they will be his peoples, and God himself will be with them; ⁴he will wipe every tear from their eyes. Death will be no more; mourning and crying and pain will be no more, for the first things have passed away."

This is just *one* of the New Testament texts that provides a glimpse of how God will fulfill God's promises of new life in a final and complete way. The rest of the book of Revelation reveals that this victory of God is not won without a struggle.

Choose one or more and explain.

■ Where do you turn when you face hardships or struggles?

a. Friend or spouse   e. Inward (inner strength)
b. Prayer   f. Extended family
c. Counselor or pastor   g. Books, poetry, music
d. Private journal   h. Other

Choose one and explain your response.

■ When you think about Jesus returning as part of God's plan to restore all creation, how do you feel?

a. anxious   e. excited
b. indifferent   f. skeptical
c. afraid   g. joyful
d. relieved   h. Other

Wrap-up

Before you go, take time for the following:

- ■ Group ministry task

- ■ Review

- ■ Personal concerns and prayer concerns

- ■ Closing prayers

Daily walk

Bible readings

Day 1
Romans 4:21

Day 2
1 John 2:25

Day 3
Romans 8:28

Day 4
Romans 8:38-39

Day 5
Revelation 21:1-2,9-14

Day 6
Revelation 21:15-21

Day 7
Revelation 21:22-27

Thought for the journey

Whatever God has promised, God has done. I can trust God's promises in my own life.

Prayer for the journey

Lord God, thank you for acting on our behalf throughout all ages. Please help us to live in harmony with your plan of salvation. In Jesus' name. Amen.

Verse for the journey

"I am about to do a new thing; now it springs forth, do you not perceive it? I will make a way in the wilderness and rivers in the desert" (Isaiah 43:19).

5 The Bible: Source of Life

Focus

The Bible provides resources for study, meditation, and prayer, which God uses to strengthen our faith and empower us for daily living.

Community building

Discuss as a group.

- ■ Consider the following question. You will not be asked to share your response with others.

  How many hours per week do you spend doing the following? Use this key: A = 0-1 hour; B = 1-2 hours; C = 2-5 hours; D = more than 5 hours.

  ___ praying   ___ reading the Bible
  ___ serving God   ___ worship
  ___ serving others

- ■ What kinds of things that you do fall under "serving God"?

- ■ Would you like to change any of the priorities you identified above? Explain. How will you do it?

Option

Look at the cup, ruler, piece of bread, light bulb, vegetable seed, and other objects that the facilitator may have provided. Choose at least one object and say, "I think the Bible is like this (your object), because . . .

The facilitator should provide a variety of objects for this activity. Use the ones listed and add more of your own.

Opening prayer
Lord, help us to order our days and our deeds according to your Word. May your Spirit help us to balance our busy lives and make more room for you. Make us aware of your presence in all we do. In Jesus' name. Amen.

Source of life

Life is precious. For Christians, God is the source of life.

Before exploring the biblical text, think about this question and discuss as a group.

■ On the most basic level, what do we need in order to survive, to remain alive? Name at least five things in order of their importance, according to your opinion.

■ Name five additional things you think we need in order for our lives to be full and rewarding.

Psalm 23:1-3

Read the biblical texts aloud and discuss.

¹ The LORD is my shepherd, I shall not want. ²He makes me lie down in green pastures; he leads me beside still waters; ³he restores my soul. He leads me in right paths for his name's sake.

John 7:37b-38

³⁷ [Jesus] . . . cried out, "Let anyone who is thirsty come to me, ³⁸and let the one who believes in me drink. As the scripture has said, 'Out of the believer's heart shall flow rivers of living water.'"

John 6:35

³⁵ Jesus said to them, "I am the bread of life. Whoever comes to me will never be hungry, and whoever believes in me will never be thirsty."

■ Compare these passages to the lists you made above. What connections do you see?

■ When describing the Bible as a "source of life," why is it important to start with the kind of images found in Psalm 23 and John 6:35; 7:37-38?

In Chapter 1, we discussed the purpose of Scripture. It reveals who God is and what God has done. It is also a means of grace, because it brings the Gospel. The Bible has been described as the "cradle" that holds Christ. John's gospel tops them all by declaring that Jesus IS the Word of God. We cannot begin to describe the Bible as a source of life apart from the One who is life. But recognizing this, we can move on to talk about how God's Word in Scripture can strengthen and sustain our faith and empower us for living.

■ In what area of your life would you like to be most empowered?

  a. Confidence in faith.
  b. Confidence in relationships.
  c. Sensitivity to the needs of others.
  d. Sense of peace and calm in the midst of hectic schedules.
  e. Courage to risk oneself on behalf of convictions or the needs of others.
  f. Ability to cooperate with others.
  g. Be more organized or disciplined in life.
  h. Courage to simplify one's lifestyle.
  i. Other.

■ How would you like—or how could you imagine—Jesus as the word of God to be the source of the empowerment you identified above?

Consider this

Discuss as a group.

"All of us need a center, a life-giving source."

■ What would you call your "center"? Explain.

A further look

You may recall discussing Psalm 1 in Chapter 3 (page 28). Read all of this short psalm again and then compare it to Jeremiah 17:5-8. Both texts include the image of trees planted beside water.

■ What or who are these trees? From what source do they draw life?

When we stay close to the word of God through regular Bible study, and close to the people of God, we will continually receive spiritual nourishment from God as a tree receives its nourishment from the nearby stream. Then we will start to yield fruit in our life. God will use us to help somebody else. Somebody else's life will be better because of God working through us. That's when life can really be exciting. That's when some people feel truly alive.

Compare with Romans 4:13-15.

■ Based on your discussion so far, what would you say is the difference between trusting in our ability to follow the law and trusting in God (the Lord) working through us?

45

Clutter!

For most of us, life is cluttered by many things—closets, hectic schedules, work, commitments, worries, health problems, and more. You name it. Even boredom or loneliness can be a form of clutter if we let it.

■ How cluttered is your life?

_____

Not at all   **Somewhat**   **Very**

■ Where would you start if you were going to unclutter your life? Why?

Matthew 14:23

23 **And after he had dismissed the crowds, [Jesus] went up the mountain by himself to pray. When evening came, he was there alone.**

Luke 11:1-4

1 **He was praying in a certain place, and after he had finished, one of his disciples said to him, "Lord, teach us to pray, as John taught his disciples." 2He said to them, "When you pray, say: Father, hallowed be your name. Your kingdom come. 3Give us each day our daily bread. 4And forgive us our sins, for we ourselves forgive everyone indebted to us. And do not bring us to the time of trial."**

Jesus' own life, especially after his earthly ministry began, was probably rather cluttered by clamoring crowds seeking his healing and miracles. Many hung on his words—some to hear their "new truth," and others to try to twist his words and challenge his authority. Like hordes of modern-day reporters trying to get a good sound bite or grab a good photo, the crowds remained close when Jesus was out in public. Sometimes it got to be too much.

- Why did Jesus go away by himself (Matthew 14:23)?

- What does this say about the importance of prayer and the benefit of prayer?

- What did the disciples request (Luke 11:1)?

- What was Jesus' response?

- The Lord's Prayer has been described as a gift that comes straight from Jesus' own mouth. How important has this prayer been in your life? Explain.

The Bible is a source of life. It teaches us how to pray and encourages us to pray. Prayer is a way we stay connected to the source of life. If we don't take time for prayer, we can experience a dry spell. The source is always there, but something—whether our own sinful nature or one of the things that clutter our lives—cuts us off. After a while we start living on less "spiritual" nourishment, less life-giving water.

- What happens to plants that don't receive enough water or nourishment?

Choose one in each pair and discuss.

- For me prayer is like . . .
  a. a dialogue/a monologue
  b. a grocery list/a song
  c. asking/receiving
  d. praising/complaining
  e. impatience/patience

Explore and relate.

Consider this

"Creating space for God within the busyness of our day reclaims the space God has already made for us."

From *'Tis a Gift to be Simple*, copyright © 1992 Augsburg Fortress.

- What is this "space"?
- How can you reclaim it?

A further look

Read and discuss.

The apostle Paul wrote: "Do not worry about anything, but in everything by prayer and supplication with thanksgiving let your requests be made known to God" (Philippians 4:6).

- How is it possible to do what Paul suggests? Does it strike you as easy or difficult? Explain.

- What needs to accompany our requests? Why is this important?

The community of believers

Besides the Word of God itself and prayer, the community of believers provides another source of life for believers. In fact, the community of believers, the church acting as Christ's body on earth, is the very place where God's Word is revealed. The church exists to preach the good news of Jesus Christ and to forgive sins; to provide the sacraments as a means of grace; and to teach the Word of God. If we are cut off from or choose to live apart from the community of believers, we are cut off from the gifts that God has given the church to provide.

Respond as a group.

■ Reflect on your experiences in the "church." Have they been positive? Negative? Some of both? Explain.

■ In your opinion, what is the most important thing the church does or provides?

1 Corinthians 12:4-13

Read the biblical text and discuss.

4 Now there are varieties of gifts, but the same Spirit; 5and there are varieties of of services, but the same Lord; 6and there are varieties of activities, but it is the same God who activates all of them in everyone. 7To each is given the manifestation of the Spirit for the common good. 8To one is given through the Spirit the utterance of wisdom, and to another the utterance of knowledge according to the same Spirit, 9to another faith by the same Spirit, to another gifts of healing by the one Spirit, 10to another the working of miracles, to another prophecy, to another the discernment of spirits, to another various kinds of tongues, to another the interpretation of tongues. 11All these are activated by one and the same Spirit, who allots to each one individually just as the Spirit chooses.

12 For just as the body is one and has many members, and all the members of the body, through many, are one body, so it is with Christ. 13For in the one Spirit we were all baptized into one body—Jews or Greeks, slaves or free—and we were all made to drink of one Spirit.

■ The body of Christ is a gifted body. According to 1 Corinthians 12:4-7, where is the focus on the gifts in the body of Christ?

Choose one or more of the following.

    a. The gifted individual.
    b. The divine gift giver.
    c. The receiver of the gifts.
    d. Other.

- What do the gifts in the body of Christ say about your value to God?

- What do the gifts say to you about the value of the body of Christ?

Many of the identified gifts relate directly to the sharing of the word of God with others (wisdom, knowledge, prophesy, discernment of spirits, tongues, and the interpretation of tongues). It is through such spiritual gifts that we can say, "Jesus is Lord" (1 Corinthians 12:3).

- How has the church, the body of Christ, communicated the word of God to you in word or deed?

- How have you communicated God's love and forgiveness to others?

- How would you like to communicate God's love and forgiveness?

The city of Corinth was known for the ecstatic expressions of its pagan cults. This background influenced the concerns and topics the apostle Paul addressed with the Corinthian church. In addition to the more dramatic gifts of miraculous faith (13:2) and the interpretation of various and unintelligible sounds (tongues), Paul can also list everyday spiritual gifts such as teaching, giving, leading, and compassion (Romans 12:7-8). No one list exhausts the variety of ways God's people are gifted to care for the common good (1 Corinthians 12:7).

- What gifts do you value in others?

- What gifts are you glad to offer the body of Christ?

- What gifts would you like to be able to offer?

Read and discuss.

Consider this

"The church is not a building . . . a committee, or a board . . ."

From "The Church Song" by Jay Beech, © 1988. All rights reserved.

- What does this line mean to you?

- How would you finish this verse?

Discuss as time allows.

- Two insights I found especially helpful in this chapter were . . .

- I really appreciated what (name of group member) said about . . .

Wrap-up

Before you go, take time for the following:

- **Group ministry task**

- **Review**

- **Personal concerns and prayer concerns**

- **Closing prayers**

Daily walk

Bible readings

Day 1
Psalm 119:47

Day 2
Psalm 119:72

Day 3
Psalm 119:97

Day 4
Deuteronomy 11:18

Day 5
Psalm 119:11

Day 6
Colossians 3:16

Day 7
Psalm 19:8

Thought for the journey

God's well is deep and available for all who want its life-giving water.

Prayer for the journey

Lord, we give thanks for your Word, for prayer, and for the community of believers. May your Spirit encourage us to receive these gifts with thanksgiving and rely on them to strengthen us in faith. In Jesus' name. Amen.

Verse for the journey

"Ho, everyone who thirsts, come to the waters" (Isaiah 55:1a).

6

The Bible: A Tool for Witness

Focus

The Bible provides a story that we are called to share with others.

Community building

Create new categories or use those suggested.

- Pair off with someone in the group and interview him or her to find out his or her:
    - a. Favorite color.
    - b. Favorite movie.
    - c. Favorite food.
    - d. Greatest joy
    - e. Biggest disappointment (response optional).
    - f. Biggest concern (personal or global).
    - g. No. 1 goal for the future.

- After a few minutes, switch roles. If time allows, report on the interviews in the large group. It may be interesting to find out which responses people had in common.

- This final chapter is about passing on God's Word, witnessing to others. Usually witnessing is thought of as "telling," but this opening activity is a reminder that the best witnessing begins with care-filled listening.

Option
When you think of the word *witnessing*, what comes to mind? Why?

■ **Share an experience of when someone "witnessed" to you. Was the experience positive? Why or why not?**

Opening prayer

God of salvation, thank you for speaking to us through your Word in Scripture. Give us wisdom and courage as we witness to the power of your forgiveness and the hope of the resurrection, which is ours through Christ Jesus our Lord. Amen.

Discovery

Before looking at the biblical texts, consider and discuss.

Christians have been referred to as the "priesthood of all believers." This description follows 1 Peter 2:9, which describes Jesus' followers as a "royal priesthood," and the book of Hebrews, in which Jesus is seen as the new high priest who replaces the priesthood based on the Law of Moses.

The priesthood of all believers emphasizes that all Christians have free and equal access to God. This privilege is not reserved for professional clergy alone. It also means that all Christians have a vital role in the ministry of the church. The church is "a chosen race, a royal priesthood, a holy nation, God's own people," and the task of this unique people is to "proclaim the mighty acts of him who called you out of darkness and into his marvelous light" (1 Peter 2:9).

- What is encouraging about being part of the priesthood of all believers?

- How might you be uncomfortable with or challenged by the concept of "priesthood of all believers"?

- What difference might such a concept make to your personal witness? To the witness strategy of a local church or national church body?

Acts 1:8

Read and discuss.

8 "But you will receive power when the Holy Spirit has come upon you; and you will be my witnesses in Jerusalem, in all Judea and Samaria, and to the ends of the earth."

Jesus made this promise to the disciples shortly before he ascended to heaven.

- What resource did Jesus say the disciples would receive that would help them "witness"?

- What did he identify as the primary purpose of the Holy Spirit?

The rest of the book of Acts tells how this promise came true. God sent the Holy Spirit as promised (Acts 2), and Jesus' small band of followers grew and organized themselves to reach out to both the Jews and Gentiles (non-Jews) in the regions of Palestine and throughout the lands that surrounded the Mediterranean Sea.

- What problems do you imagine the earliest apostles faced while trying to tell the good news about Jesus?

■ What problems do those who witness to the good news face today? What advantages do modern-day witnesses have?

Read and discuss.

Consider this

"The best witnesses have large ears and small mouths."

■ Do you agree with this? Why or why not?

A further look
Read and discuss.

Philip was appointed to be one of the early church leaders (see Acts 6:5). Leaders like Philip were appointed to help take care of the everyday concerns of the believers so the apostles would be free to concentrate on teaching, preaching, and working miracles. But Philip became a witness in his own right. Read about his encounter with an Ethiopian court official in Acts 8:26-39.

■ What evidence is there in the story that this Ethiopian was a Jewish proselyte (a non-Jew who had followed the Jewish religion)? See 8:27-28 for two clues.

■ How did Philip begin his conversation with the Ethiopian?

■ What was the Ethiopian reading? What was his question?

■ What did Philip use to proclaim the good news?

■ What did Philip's witness prompt the man to ask (8:37)?

Choose one in each pair and explain.

■ Would you describe Philip as . . .
  a. pushy/responsive   c. unprepared/prepared
  b. open/closed   d. exclusive/inclusive

■ What can be learned about witnessing from this story?

Discovery

Good news

Explore and relate.

■ What is the best news you have ever received?

■ How did this news come to you?

■ In your experience, how does good news usually get passed on?

Romans 10:13-17

Read the text aloud and
discuss.

13 For, "Everyone who calls on the name of the Lord shall be saved." 14 But how are they to call on one in whom they have not believed? And how are they to believe in one of whom they have never heard? And how are they to hear without someone to proclaim him? 15 And how are they to proclaim him unless they are sent? As it is written, "How beautiful are the feet of those who bring good news!" 16 But not all have obeyed the good news; for Isaiah says, "Lord, who has believed our message?" 17 So faith comes from what is heard, and what is heard comes through the word of Christ.

Paul made a simple but powerful argument about witnessing in this passage. Following through on his comments, however, seems to be easier said than done.

- Verse 13 reveals God's will, which is for all people (10:12). What does God want?

- How, according to Paul, can this happen?

- How is faith created (see 10:17)?

- Not everyone can be a preacher. How else can we "proclaim" the good news?

- Think about the following groups. How easy or difficult is it for you to talk about your faith with them?

Circle your responses
and discuss.

Group	Easy				Hard
Family members	1	2	3	4	5
Friends	1	2	3	4	5
Coworkers	1	2	3	4	5
Acquaintances	1	2	3	4	5
Spouse	1	2	3	4	5
Strangers	1	2	3	4	5

If your total score is 18-30, you are not alone. Brainstorm together about ways that you can become more comfortable sharing your faith, proclaiming the good news.

Spend some time in
pairs or groups of three
sharing your faith sto-
ries. This activity may
take some time. Will
you need to add time to
your session or divide it
into two periods?

- Remember, the Bible is the "story" of God and God's relationship to people. What is the "story" of your relationship with God, your faith story? Spend a few minutes writing down some key points in this story. Think about:
  a. How did the story begin?
  b. What are the important events in the plot?
  c. Has there been a turning point yet?
  d. Who are the main characters?
  e. Where is the story going next?
  f. Have you considered how the story will end?

A further look
Read and discuss.

In 1 Corinthians 9:22-23, the apostle Paul wrote, "I have become all things to all people, that I might by all means save some. I do it all for the sake of the gospel, so that I may share in its blessings." You may wish to read all of 1 Corinthians 9 to understand Paul's words in context.

■ What do you think it means to be all things to all people for the sake of the gospel?

Choose one and explain.

    a. It's OK to be wishy-washy about my standards.

    b. I practice the art of empathy, trying to put myself in another person's shoes.

    c. I change my beliefs to make others happy.

    d. I live with others while trying to be sensitive to their lifestyles and values as much as possible.

    e. Other.

■ Who or what has influenced your faith the most? Why?

List all responses.

■ Name some qualities that describe a "faithful witness"?

Discovery

A picture is worth . . .

Play a quick game of charades. One volunteer stands and acts out the name of a song, TV show, movie, or Bible story. Give the category and then give clues using only actions and no words whatsoever. Other volunteers can take a turn as time allows.

Discuss as a group.

■ Some people respond more to pictures or actions than to words. Which usually has more impact on you—words or actions? Why?

■ Many people today grew up with television. How might this fact influence how we choose to witness to the good news? What does or could it mean for preaching and teaching the Bible?

Romans 12:2,9-17

Read the text aloud and discuss.

2 Do not be conformed to this world, but be transformed by the renewing of your minds, so that you may discern what is the will of God—what is good and acceptable and perfect.

9 Let love be genuine; hate what is evil, hold fast to what is good; 10love one another with mutual affection; outdo one another in showing honor. 11Do not lag in zeal, be ardent in spirit, serve the Lord. 12Rejoice in hope, be patient in suffering, persevere in prayer. 13Contribute to the needs of the saints; extend hospitality to strangers.

14 Bless those who persecute you; bless and do not curse them. 15Rejoice with those who rejoice, weep with those who weep. 16Live in harmony with one another; do not be haughty, but associate with the lowly; do not claim to be wiser than you are. 17Do not repay anyone evil for evil, but take thought for what is noble in the sight of all.

Paul established in his letter to the Romans that we are saved by God's undeserved kindness through the death and resurrection of Christ Jesus (3:24). What we do or how well we keep God's laws will never be a way to gain salvation. That doesn't mean we disregard the laws of God, we uphold them (3:31). We do this not in order to be saved, but because we are already saved. We allow God's Spirit to transform us, remake us, from the inside out. When Paul talks about the transformed life in 12:2, he is not suggesting that we manipulate ourselves into a right relationship with God, but that we open ourselves to the Spirit, who is already at work in our lives.

- Why did Paul say, "Do not be conformed to this world"?

- How does our world try to mold us into its image?

- Animals and plants that are similar in species are often identified or distinguished from others by their unique "markings." According to Paul, what are some of the "markings" of a Christian (12:9-17)?

- Do you know of anyone who has displayed these Christian markings?

- How do you think people in your community view the local Christian community? Why? Are the "markings" that Paul talked about easily visible to those inside or outside the congregation? Explain.

Read and discuss.

Consider this

Consider the statement, "Love is a verb."

- Do you agree that the word *love* has lost some of its meaning today? Explain.

- Why is it important to think of love as a verb? What does this have to do with witnessing?

As you bring this study to a close, consider the following:

- Name two new insights you have had. Why are they significant?

- Where do you go from here? Are there topics you touched on that you want to explore together in greater depth in the future?

- What difference has this study made in your understanding of the Bible? How may it affect how you use the Bible? Do you have or will you make plans to do further personal and group study of the Bible?

A further look

Read Colossians 3:12-17 twice, once to yourself and once with volunteers slowly reading it aloud.

- What major themes in this small group exploration of *The Bible and Life* are contained in this passage? Explain.

- Share a theme that is of particular importance or interest to you.

Wrap-up

Before you go, take time for the following:

- Group ministry task

- Review

- Personal concerns and prayer concerns

- Closing prayers

Daily walk

Bible readings

Day 1
Exodus 4:12

Day 2
Matthew 10:19

Day 3
Luke 21:15

Day 4
1 Corinthians 13:4-7

Day 5
1 John 4:15

Day 6
Jeremiah 1:9

Day 7
Matthew 10:32

Thought for the journey

Every conversation is an opportunity for telling the Jesus story in word and deed.

Prayer for the journey

Dear Lord, as you sent someone to me to lead me to your Word, please prepare me and send me to others as a witness to the good news. In Jesus' name. Amen.

Verse for the journey

"And remember, I am with you always, to the end of the age" (Matthew 28:20b).

Appendix

Group directory

Record information about group members here.

Names   **Addresses**   **Phone Numbers**

_____

_____

_____

_____

_____

_____

_____

_____

_____

_____

Group commitments

"Do not be conformed to this world, but be transformed by the renewing of your minds, so that you may discern what is the will of God—what is good and acceptable and perfect" (Romans 12:2).

■ For our time together, we have made the following commitments to each other

■ Goals for our study of this topic are

■ Our group ministry task is

■ My personal action plan is

Prayer requests

Prayers

■ Closing Prayer

Lord God, you have called your servants to ventures of which we cannot see the ending, by paths as yet untrodden, through perils unknown. Give us faith to go out with good courage, not knowing where we go, but only that your hand is leading us and your love supporting us; through Jesus Christ our Lord. Amen.

Lutheran Book of Worship, copyright © 1978, 153.

(If you plan to use the Lord's Prayer, record the version your group uses in the next column.)

■ The Lord's Prayer

Resources

Aaseng, Rolf E. *A Beginner's Guide to Studying the Bible.* Minneapolis: Augsburg Fortress, 1991.

Jacobson, Diane L., and Kysar, Robert. *A Beginner's Guide to Books of the Bible.* Minneapolis: Augsburg Fortress, 1991.

Koester, Craig R. *A Beginner's Guide to Reading the Bible.* Minneapolis: Augsburg Fortress, 1991.

Please tell us about your experience with INTERSECTIONS.

4. What I like best about my INTERSECTIONS experience is

5. Three things I want to see the same in future INTERSECTIONS books are

6. Three things I might change in future INTERSECTIONS books are

7. Topics I would like developed for new INTERSECTIONS books are

8. Our group had _____ sessions for the six chapters of this book

9. Other comments I have about INTERSECTIONS are

Thank you for taking the time to fill out and return this questionnaire.

---------------------------FOLD CARD IN HERE, SEAL WITH TAPE, AND MAIL TODAY!-------------------

Please check the INTERSECTIONS book you are evaluating.

☐ Following Jesus   ☐ Death and Grief   ☐ Men and Women
☐ The Bible and Life   ☐ Divorce   ☐ Peace
☐ Captive and Free   ☐ Faith   ☐ Praying
☐ Caring and Community   ☐ Jesus: Divine and Human   ☐ Self-Esteem

Please tell us about your small group.

1. Our group had an average attendance of _____.

2. Our group was made up of
   _____ Young adults (19-25 years)
   _____ Adults (most between 25-45 years)
   _____ Adults (most between 45-60 years)
   _____ Adults (most between 60-75 years)
   _____ Adults (most 75 and over)
   _____ Adults (wide mix of ages)
   _____ Men (number) and _____ women (number)

3. Our group (answer as many as apply)
   _____ came together for the sole purpose of studying this INTERSECTIONS book.
   _____ has decided to study another INTERSECTIONS book.
   _____ is an ongoing Sunday school group.
   _____ met at a time other than Sunday morning.
   _____ had only one facilitator for this study.

BUSINESS REPLY MAIL

FIRST-CLASS MAIL   PERMIT NO. 22120   MINNEAPOLIS, MN

POSTAGE WILL BE PAID BY ADDRESSEE

Augsburg Fortress

ATTN INTERSECTIONS TEAM
PO BOX 1209
MINNEAPOLIS MN 55440-8807